✪ American Girl®

Cupcakes

Photography **Nicole Hill Gerulat**

weldon**owen**

Contents

Cupcake Fun for Everyone!

Vanilla, chocolate, filled, or frosted—we love cupcakes! Not only are they exciting to eat, but they are also super fun to bake—and decorate. Invite friends over after school or on the weekend to have a decorating party. Choose a few of your favorite recipes, bake them together, and then divide and conquer the frostings and decorations. Everyone's creativity will shine through, and you'll have plenty of treats to eat at the end of the party.

A moist cake layer and a smooth frosting or glaze are important, so be sure to check out our tips for baking (page 9) and decorating (page 15). The right tools are key—you don't need many, but it's important to have a few essentials on hand before you get started. Decorating is the fun stuff! Throughout this book, we give oodles of ideas, but use your imagination. There are endless combos of frosting flavors, sprinkles, and other fun toppings to play with.

From classics, such as Yellow Cupcakes with Chocolate Frosting (page 27) and Devil's Food Cupcakes with Rich Chocolate Glaze (page 18), to creamy and crunchy Cookies 'n' Cream Cupcakes (page 61) and sprinkle-filled Piñata Cupcakes (page 76), we have a recipe for everyone. Whatever your style—whether you're daring, playful, colorful, or classic—baking is a great way to express your own special flair. And last but not least, don't forget the sprinkles!

Tip-top baking tips

★ Many of the recipes in this book use an electric mixer to mix ingredients together. Hand mixers are convenient and easy to use, but you could use a stand mixer as well. Be sure to turn off the mixer in between adding ingredients, and scrape down the bowl with a rubber spatula occasionally, to keep the mess to a minimum.

★ Butter should be at room temperature for most of the recipes in this book, since it is easier to work with in its softened state. Eggs will mix into a batter more evenly if they are at room temperature, but it's not critical for the recipe to work properly.

★ Some ingredients need to be folded into the batter instead of beaten with a mixer. When combining two mixtures of different consistencies, folding helps blend them without deflating the batter. Use a rubber spatula for this task.

★ When you think the cupcakes are done, stick a clean toothpick into the center. If it comes out clean, the cupcakes are ready. If it comes out with batter on it, they need more baking time.

★ Be sure to wait for your cupcakes to cool completely before you frost them, or the frosting might melt and drip off of them.

The tools you'll need

★ **Measuring cups and spoons** help you measure ingredients accurately and easily. Choose graduated sets for dry ingredients and a liquid pitcher for wet ingredients.

★ **Rubber spatulas, whisks, and wooden spoons** are helpful for mixing batters and folding ingredients, food coloring, and sprinkles into batters and frostings.

★ **An electric mixer** is handy for making batters and frostings and for beating egg whites.

★ **Oven mitts or pads** protect your hands from hot pans, oven racks, muffin pans, and cookie sheets.

★ **An ice cream scoop** is helpful for dividing batter evenly into muffin pans.

★ **A piping bag** fitted with a pastry tip is a fun and pretty way to frost cupcakes.

★ **Pastry tips** come in a variety of sizes and shapes, including plain, star, petal, and leaf.

★ **Small metal icing spatulas** are good for spreading frosting on cupcakes and transferring hot cupcakes to a wire rack.

★ **Rimmed cookie sheets**, especially thick ones, are useful for toasting coconut and transporting cupcakes while they are cooling.

Baking with care

Adults have lots of culinary wisdom, and can help keep you safe in the kitchen. Always have an adult assist you, especially if your recipe involves high heat, hot ovens, sharp objects, and electric appliances.

This symbol appears throughout the book to remind you that you'll need an adult to help you with all or part of the recipe. Ask for help before continuing.

The best part of cupcake making is decorating. Gather an assortment of colorful liners, sprinkles, and food coloring for a big batch of creativity!

Cupcake decorating 101

★ Cupcake liners are available in a variety of colors and patterns. If you're feeling festive, match your liners to the colors in your frosting and/or sprinkles.

★ Sprinkles come in all different shapes, colors, and sizes. We provide suggestions for which to use in some recipes, but let your imagination run wild and choose whichever you like. Keep in mind that some might bleed when added to batter, so be careful when folding them in.

★ Piping tips for pastry bags come in many shapes and sizes. Each tip is labeled with a number—the smaller the number, the smaller the hole. It's useful to have at least one plain and one star-shaped tip on hand to create different decorations.

★ To fill a pastry bag, firmly push a piping tip down into the small hole at the bottom of the bag. Form a cuff by folding down the top one-third of the bag. Place one hand under the cuff. Using a rubber spatula, scoop the frosting into the bag with your other hand, filling the bag halfway. Unfold the cuff, push the frosting down toward the tip, and twist the bag closed where the frosting ends. Squeeze the bag from the top when you pipe.

★ If you'd like to use the same frosting to pipe different shapes, use a coupler attachment on your piping bag so you can change tips easily.

Favorite Cupcakes

Devil's Food Cupcakes

These moist cupcakes have a slightly richer texture than the Chocolate Cupcakes on page 25 and are a great match for a decadent chocolate glaze. Sugared flowers are surprisingly simple to make and are a pretty way to dress up treats for a special day.

MAKES 12 CUPCAKES

1 cup all-purpose flour

¼ cup unsweetened cocoa powder, sifted

¾ teaspoon baking soda

¼ teaspoon salt

½ cup granulated sugar

½ cup firmly packed light brown sugar

4 tablespoons (½ stick) unsalted butter, at room temperature

1 large egg

1 teaspoon vanilla extract

½ cup lukewarm water

¼ cup buttermilk

Rich Chocolate Glaze (page 114)

Sugared Flowers (page 120; optional)

Step 1: Preheat the oven to 350°F. Line a standard 12-cup muffin pan with paper or foil liners.

Step 2: In a medium bowl, whisk together the flour, cocoa powder, baking soda, and salt. In a large bowl, using an electric mixer, beat the granulated sugar, brown sugar, and butter on medium-high speed until light and fluffy, 2 to 3 minutes. Add the egg and vanilla and beat until combined. Turn off the mixer and scrape down the bowl with a rubber spatula. Add about one-third of the flour mixture and mix on low speed just until blended. Pour in about half of the water and about half of the buttermilk and mix on low speed just until combined. Add about half of the remaining flour mixture and mix on low speed just until blended. Pour in the remaining water and buttermilk and mix just until combined. Add the remaining flour mixture and mix just until blended. Turn off the mixer, scrape down the bowl, and give the batter a final stir with the spatula.

Step 3: Divide the batter evenly among the prepared muffin cups. Bake until a toothpick inserted into the center of a cupcake comes out clean, 18 to 20 minutes. Remove the pan from the oven and set it on a wire rack. Let cool for 10 minutes, then carefully transfer the cupcakes directly to the rack. Let cool completely, about 1 hour.

Step 4: Spoon the chocolate glaze over the cupcakes and decorate the cupcakes with sugared flowers (if using).

Toasted Coconut Cupcakes

If you love coconut, these cupcakes are for you. Toasting brings out coconut's sweet flavor and adds a pretty golden-brown tint to these scrumptious little cakes. Sprinkle toasted coconut on top of the frosting for a fun, easy, and delicious decoration.

MAKES 12 CUPCAKES

2 cups sweetened shredded coconut

1½ cups all-purpose flour

1¼ teaspoons baking powder

¼ teaspoon salt

¾ cup plus 2 tablespoons sugar

½ cup (1 stick) unsalted butter, at room temperature

1 large egg plus
1 large egg white

1 teaspoon vanilla extract

½ cup canned coconut milk

Fluffy Vanilla Frosting or Fluffy Coconut Frosting (page 104)

 Preheat the oven to 350°F. Line a rimmed cookie sheet with parchment paper. Line a standard 12-cup muffin pan with paper or foil liners.

Spread the coconut in an even layer on the prepared cookie sheet. Bake until the coconut is golden brown at the edges, 5 to 7 minutes. Remove from the oven, set on a wire rack, and let cool completely.

In a medium bowl, whisk together the flour, baking powder, salt, and 1 cup of the toasted coconut. In a large bowl, using an electric mixer, beat the sugar and butter on medium-high speed until light and fluffy, 2 to 3 minutes. Add the egg, egg white, and vanilla and beat until combined. Turn off the mixer and scrape down the bowl with a rubber spatula. Add half of the flour mixture and mix on low speed just until blended. Pour in the coconut milk and mix on low speed just until combined. Add the remaining flour mixture and mix on low speed just until blended. Turn off the mixer and scrape down the bowl. Divide the batter evenly among the prepared muffin cups. Bake until the tops are light golden brown and a toothpick inserted into the center of a cupcake comes out clean, 18 to 20 minutes. Remove the pan from the oven and set it on a wire rack. Let cool for 10 minutes, then carefully transfer the cupcakes directly to the rack. Let cool completely, about 1 hour.

Using a small icing spatula or a butter knife, or a pastry bag fitted with a large plain tip (see page 15), top the cupcakes with the frosting. Sprinkle with the remaining toasted coconut, dividing it evenly.

Snow White Cupcakes

All-white decorations on snowy mounds of frosting give these vanilla cupcakes an angelic look, but if you like, use bold, colorful sprinkles instead. Buttermilk in the batter makes them super moist and tender.

MAKES 18 CUPCAKES

2 cups all-purpose flour

2 teaspoons baking powder

½ teaspoon baking soda

½ teaspoon salt

½ cup plus 2 tablespoons (1¼ sticks) unsalted butter, at room temperature

1 cup sugar

2 large eggs

2 teaspoons vanilla extract

1⅓ cups buttermilk

Fluffy Vanilla Frosting (page 104)

Edible white pearl beads and/or white sanding sugar, for decorating

 Preheat the oven to 375°F. Line 18 cups of two standard muffin pans with paper or foil liners.

In a medium bowl, whisk together the flour, baking powder, baking soda, and salt. In a large bowl, using an electric mixer, beat the butter and sugar on medium-high speed until light and fluffy, 2 to 3 minutes. Add the eggs one at a time, beating well after each addition. Turn off the mixer and scrape down the bowl with a rubber spatula. Add the vanilla and beat until combined. Turn off the mixer. Add about half of the flour mixture and mix on low speed just until blended. Pour in the buttermilk and mix on low speed until combined. Add the remaining flour mixture and mix just until blended. Turn off the mixer, scrape down the bowl, and give the batter a final stir with the spatula. The batter will be thick.

Divide the batter evenly among the prepared muffin cups. Bake until the tops are light golden brown and a toothpick inserted into the center of a cupcake comes out clean, about 17 minutes. Remove the pans from the oven and set them on a wire rack. Let cool for 10 minutes, then carefully transfer the cupcakes directly to the rack. Let cool completely, about 1 hour.

Using a small icing spatula or a butter knife, or a pastry bag fitted with a large plain tip (see page 15), top the cupcakes with the frosting, then decorate them with edible beads and/or sparkling sugar.

Sweet swoops
Use a small icing spatula to create the soft, natural-looking swirls of frosting on these cupcakes.

Chocolate Cupcakes

A double dose of chocolate—in the form of cocoa powder and bittersweet chocolate—makes these cupcakes extra rich. This recipe includes instructions for piping flowers, but you can pipe a different design, or just spread on the frosting with an icing spatula.

MAKES 12 CUPCAKES

⅔ cup all-purpose flour

2½ tablespoons unsweetened cocoa powder, sifted

¾ teaspoon baking powder

¼ teaspoon salt

½ cup (1 stick) plus 3 tablespoons unsalted butter, cut into pieces

3 ounces bittersweet chocolate, chopped

¾ cup plus 2 tablespoons sugar

3 large eggs

1 teaspoon vanilla extract

Fluffy Vanilla Frosting (page 104)

Yellow gel paste food coloring

Step 1: Preheat the oven to 350°F. Line a standard 12-cup muffin pan with paper or foil liners.

Step 2: In a medium bowl, whisk together the flour, cocoa powder, baking powder, and salt.

Step 3: In a medium microwave-safe bowl, combine the butter and chocolate. Microwave on high power, stirring every 20 seconds, just until the mixture is melted and smooth. Let the mixture cool until barely warm, 10 to 15 minutes.

Step 4: Add the sugar to the chocolate mixture and stir with a whisk until combined. Add the eggs one at a time, whisking until well combined after each addition. Add the vanilla and mix until blended. Add the flour mixture and mix just until combined and no traces of flour remain; do not overmix.

Step 5: Divide the batter evenly among the prepared muffin cups. Bake until a toothpick inserted into the center of a cupcake comes out with only a few crumbs attached, 22 to 24 minutes. Remove the pan from the oven and set it on a wire rack. Let cool for 10 minutes, then carefully transfer the cupcakes directly to the rack. Let cool completely, about 1 hour.

~ *Continued on page 26* ~

Bright blossoms
Be creative and use any color combo for your flowers. Try bright petals paired with white or yellow centers.

~ *Continued from page 25* ~

Step 6: To pipe flowers on the cupcakes, place about one-fourth of the frosting in a small bowl, add 2 dabs of yellow food coloring, and mix with a rubber spatula until the frosting is evenly tinted. Fit a pastry bag with a small round tip (see page 15), then transfer the yellow frosting to the bag; set aside. Fit another pastry bag with a petal tip, then transfer the remaining white frosting to the bag.

Step 7: Pipe white petals by positioning the petal tip horizontally with the wide end in the center of the cupcake, then, while gently squeezing the bag, make a half-moon motion with the outer, thinner edge of the tip. Pipe another petal slightly overlapping the first one. Repeat until petals cover the top of the cupcake. Use the piping bag with yellow frosting to pipe a yellow center on the flower. Decorate the remaining cupcakes in the same way.

Yellow Cupcakes

These cupcakes are the classic choice for birthday parties, but they're perfect for any occasion. Choose between a gooey chocolate frosting and a smooth chocolate glaze, then decorate them with oodles of sprinkles.

MAKES 24 CUPCAKES

2¾ cups cake flour

1 tablespoon baking powder

½ teaspoon salt

1 cup (2 sticks) unsalted butter, at room temperature

1¾ cups sugar

4 large eggs plus 2 large egg yolks

2 teaspoons vanilla extract

1 cup sour cream

Chocolate Frosting (page 113) or Rich Chocolate Glaze (page 114)

Sprinkles, for decorating (optional)

Step 1: Preheat the oven to 350°F. Line 24 cups of two standard muffin pans with paper or foil liners.

Step 2: In a medium bowl, whisk together the flour, baking powder, and salt. In a large bowl, using an electric mixer, beat the butter and sugar on medium-high speed until light and fluffy, 2 to 3 minutes. Add the eggs and yolks one at a time, beating well after each addition. Turn off the mixer and scrape down the bowl with a rubber spatula. Add the vanilla and beat until combined. Add about half of the flour mixture and mix on low speed just until blended. Add the sour cream and mix on low speed just until combined. Add the remaining flour mixture and mix just until blended.

Step 3: Divide the batter evenly among the prepared muffin cups. Bake until the tops are light golden brown and a toothpick inserted into the center of a cupcake comes out clean, 22 to 24 minutes. Remove the pans from the oven and set them on a wire rack. Let cool for 10 minutes, then carefully transfer the cupcakes directly to the rack. Let cool completely, about 1 hour.

Step 4: If decorating the cupcakes with chocolate frosting, use a small icing spatula or a butter knife, or a pastry bag fitted with a plain or star tip (see page 15), top the cupcakes with the frosting, then decorate them with sprinkles (if using). If glazing the cupcakes, spoon the chocolate glaze over the cupcakes, then decorate them with sprinkles (if using).

Chocolate-Banana Cream Pie Cupcakes

Banana cupcakes filled with vanilla cream and topped with chocolate glaze? Yes, please! For the best taste and texture, make sure your bananas are nice and ripe—they should be spotty brown and a little soft to the touch.

MAKES 18 CUPCAKES

BANANA CUPCAKES

2 cups all-purpose flour

2 teaspoons baking powder

½ teaspoon baking soda

½ teaspoon salt

½ cup (1 stick) unsalted butter, at room temperature

1¼ cups sugar

2 large eggs

1 teaspoon vanilla extract

2 ripe bananas, peeled and mashed (about 1 cup)

½ cup buttermilk

Vanilla Custard (page 117)

Rich Chocolate Glaze (page 114)

Chunk of dark chocolate, for decorating (optional)

 To make the cupcakes, preheat the oven to 350°F. Line 18 cups of two standard muffin pans with paper or foil liners.

In a medium bowl, whisk together the flour, baking powder, baking soda, and salt. In a large bowl, using an electric mixer, beat the butter and sugar on medium-high speed until light and fluffy, 2 to 3 minutes. Add the eggs one at a time, beating well after each addition. Turn off the mixer and scrape down the bowl with a rubber spatula. Add the vanilla and bananas and beat until combined.

Turn off the mixer. Add half of the flour mixture and mix on low speed just until blended. Pour in the buttermilk and mix on low speed just until combined. Add the remaining flour mixture and mix on low speed just until blended. Turn off the mixer, scrape down the bowl, and give the batter a final stir with the spatula.

Divide the batter evenly among the prepared muffin cups. Bake until light golden brown and a toothpick inserted into the center of a cupcake comes out clean, 18 to 20 minutes. Remove the pan from the oven and set it on a wire rack. Let cool for 10 minutes, then carefully transfer the cupcakes directly to the rack. Let cool completely, about 1 hour.

~ *Continued on page 32* ~

Cool cupcakes

These cream-filled treats taste yummy straight from the refrigerator—no need to let them warm up before munching.

~ *Continued from page 31* ~

Using a paring knife, cut a 1½-inch-diameter round about 1 inch deep in the center of each cupcake, then remove the rounds and set them aside. Fill each hollow with about 1 teaspoon of vanilla custard. Cut the rounds that you removed from the cupcakes in half horizontally; reserve the tops and discard—or eat!—the rest. Return the tops to the cupcakes, covering the filling, then gently press down on each to fit it into the hole.

Spoon the chocolate glaze over the cupcakes. If decorating with chocolate, use a vegetable peeler to shave the chunk of chocolate over the cupcakes, letting the shavings fall onto the glaze. Place the cupcakes on a rimmed baking sheet and refrigerate until the glaze is set, about 10 minutes.

Chocolate Éclair Cupcakes

Follow the recipe for Chocolate-Banana Cream Pie Cupcakes, swapping Vanilla Cupcakes (page 36; omit the frosting and sprinkles) for the Banana Cupcakes.

Carrot Cake Cupcakes

Carrots and cinnamon are a great combo for baking, especially in cupcakes topped with cream cheese frosting, the classic and totally scrumptious match for carrot cake. You can use the small holes of a box grater (the kind used for cheese) to finely grate the carrots.

MAKES 12 CUPCAKES

1½ cups all-purpose flour

1 teaspoon baking powder

½ teaspoon baking soda

½ teaspoon salt

½ teaspoon ground cinnamon

1 cup sugar

¾ cup vegetable oil

2 large eggs

¼ cup buttermilk

½ teaspoon vanilla extract

3 carrots, peeled and finely grated (1½ cups)

Cream Cheese Frosting (page 108)

 Preheat the oven to 350°F. Line a standard 12-cup muffin pan with paper or foil liners.

In a medium bowl, whisk together the flour, baking powder, baking soda, salt, and cinnamon. In a large bowl, whisk together the sugar, oil, eggs, buttermilk, and vanilla until well combined. Add the carrots and whisk until evenly moistened. Add the flour mixture and fold with a rubber spatula until the batter is well blended.

Divide the batter evenly among the prepared muffin cups. Bake until the tops are golden brown and a toothpick inserted into the center of a cupcake comes out clean, 20 to 25 minutes. Remove the pan from the oven and set it on a wire rack. Let cool for 10 minutes, then carefully transfer the cupcakes directly to the rack. Let cool completely, about 1 hour.

Using a small icing spatula or a butter knife, or a pastry bag fitted with a large plain or star tip (see page 15), top the cupcakes with the frosting.

Pink Velvet Cupcakes

This playful and pretty take on red velvet cake is flavored with strawberries inside and on top. Freeze-dried strawberries are sold in the same aisle as the dried fruits and nuts in most grocery stores, but if you can't find any, increase the flour in the batter to 2½ cups.

MAKES 20 CUPCAKES

2 tablespoons unsweetened cocoa powder, sifted

⅓ cup boiling water

1 cup buttermilk

1 cup freeze-dried strawberries

2 cups all-purpose flour

¼ teaspoon salt

¾ cup (1½ sticks) unsalted butter, at room temperature

1½ cups sugar

3 large eggs

2 teaspoons vanilla extract

Pink gel paste food coloring

1½ teaspoons baking soda

1 teaspoon white vinegar

Double recipe Strawberry–Cream Cheese Frosting (page 108)

Red, pink, and heart-shaped sprinkles, for decorating (optional)

Preheat the oven to 350°F. Line 20 cups of two standard 12-cup muffin pans with paper or foil liners.

In a medium heatproof bowl, whisk the cocoa and boiling water until well combined, then whisk in the buttermilk. Set aside.

Place the strawberries in a quart-size zipper-lock bag and seal the bag. Using a rolling pin or wooden spoon, crush the strawberries to a fine powder. In a small bowl, whisk together the flour, salt, and strawberry powder.

In a large bowl, using an electric mixer, beat the butter and sugar on medium speed until light and fluffy, 2 to 3 minutes. Add the eggs one at a time, beating well after each addition. Add the vanilla and 3 dabs of food coloring and beat until combined. Add half of the flour mixture and mix on low speed just until blended. Pour in the cocoa-buttermilk mixture and mix on low speed until combined. Add the remaining flour mixture and beat just until blended. In a small bowl, stir together the baking soda and vinegar, then quickly add the mixture to the batter and stir with a rubber spatula until combined.

Divide the batter evenly among the prepared muffin cups. Bake until a toothpick inserted into the center of a cupcake comes out clean, about 18 minutes. Remove the pans from the oven and let cool on a wire rack for 10 minutes, then transfer the cupcakes to the rack to cool completely, about 1 hour.

Using a pastry bag fitted with a star tip (see page 15), frost the cupcakes, then decorate them with sprinkles (if using).

Vanilla Cupcakes

These cupcakes are the perfect base for many of the recipes in this book. To make the orange- and yellow-hued flower design on pages 38–39, follow the directions in the box on page 37. Or get creative and tint the frosting colors any way you like.

MAKES 12 CUPCAKES

1¼ cups all-purpose flour

1¼ teaspoons baking powder

¼ teaspoon salt

¾ cup sugar

6 tablespoons (¾ stick) unsalted butter, at room temperature

2 large eggs

1 teaspoon vanilla extract

⅓ cup whole milk

Fluffy Vanilla Frosting (page 104)

Sprinkles and/or candies, for decorating

Step 1: Preheat the oven to 350°F. Line a standard 12-cup muffin pan with paper or foil liners.

Step 2: In a medium bowl, whisk together the flour, baking powder, and salt. In a large bowl, using an electric mixer, beat the sugar and butter on medium-high speed until light and fluffy, 2 to 3 minutes. Add the eggs one at a time, beating well after each addition. Turn off the mixer and scrape down the bowl with a rubber spatula. Add the vanilla and beat until combined. Add about half of the flour mixture and mix on low speed just until blended. Add the milk and mix on low speed until combined. Add the remaining flour mixture and mix just until blended. Turn off the mixer, scrape down the bowl, and give the batter a final stir with the spatula.

Step 3: Divide the batter evenly among the prepared muffin cups. Bake until the tops are light golden brown and a toothpick inserted into the center of a cupcake comes out clean, 18 to 20 minutes. Remove the pan from the oven and set it on a wire rack. Let cool for 10 minutes, then carefully transfer the cupcakes directly to the rack. Let cool completely, about 1 hour.

Step 4: Using a small icing spatula or a butter knife, or a pastry bag fitted with a plain or star tip (see page 15), top the cupcakes with the frosting, then decorate them with sprinkles and/or candies.

Cupcake Flowers

To create the flower design on pages 38–39, make four batches of Vanilla Cupcakes, for a total of 48 cupcakes, as well as four batches of Fluffy Vanilla Frosting (page 104), placing each batch of frosting in a medium bowl. Add 1 dab of orange food coloring to one bowl, 1 dab of yellow food coloring to the second bowl, 2 dabs of red food coloring to the third bowl, and 1 dab of green food coloring to the fourth bowl. Using a rubber spatula for each color, mix in the food coloring until the frosting is evenly tinted. With a small icing spatula or a butter knife, frost 12 of the cupcakes with the orange frosting, 12 cupcakes with the yellow frosting, 18 cupcakes with the red frosting, and the remaining 6 cupcakes with green frosting. Sprinkle 6 of the red cupcakes with mini chocolate chips so that the chips completely cover the frosting.

On a clean large board or directly on a table covered with craft paper or a washable tablecloth, arrange 6 yellow cupcakes around 1 chocolate chip–covered cupcake at the center, to form a flower design. Arrange the remaining yellow cupcakes, along with the orange cupcakes and the red cupcakes, in the same way, staggering the placement of the "flowers" and alternating their colors. Fit a pastry bag with a large plain tip and fill the bag with the remaining green frosting. Pipe lines of green frosting to resemble stems. Arrange the green cupcakes next to the stems to resemble leaves.

Gingerbread Cupcakes

As these cupcakes bake, they'll fill your kitchen with the amazing aroma of sweet, warm spices. You'll need a small snowflake cookie cutter to make a wintry design on these tasty treats, but if you don't have one, decorate the glazed cupcakes with sprinkles as you like.

MAKES 12 CUPCAKES

1¼ cups all-purpose flour

1¼ teaspoons baking powder

¼ teaspoon salt

1 teaspoon ground ginger

1 teaspoon ground cinnamon

¼ teaspoon ground allspice

Pinch of ground nutmeg

½ cup firmly packed light brown sugar

⅓ cup light molasses

4 tablespoons (½ stick) unsalted butter, at room temperature

1 large egg

2 teaspoons grated fresh ginger

⅓ cup whole milk

Lemon Glaze (page 114)

Blue sprinkles or sanding sugar, for decorating

 Preheat the oven to 350°F. Line a standard 12-cup muffin pan with paper or foil liners.

In a medium bowl, whisk together the flour, baking powder, salt, ground ginger, cinnamon, allspice, and nutmeg. In a large bowl, using an electric mixer, beat the brown sugar, molasses, and butter on medium-high speed until light and fluffy, 2 to 3 minutes. Add the egg and fresh ginger and beat until combined. Turn off the mixer and scrape down the bowl with a rubber spatula. Add about half of the flour mixture and mix on low speed just until blended. Pour in the milk and mix on low speed until combined. Add the remaining flour mixture and mix just until blended. Turn off the mixer, scrape down the bowl, and give the batter a final stir with the spatula.

Divide the batter evenly among the prepared muffin cups. Bake until a toothpick inserted into the center of a cupcake comes out clean, 20 to 22 minutes. Remove the pan from the oven and set it on a wire rack. Let cool for 10 minutes, then carefully transfer the cupcakes directly to the rack. Let cool completely, about 1 hour.

Spoon the glaze onto the cupcakes and let dry for about 5 minutes. Place a small snowflake cookie cutter on top of a cupcake and carefully pour sprinkles or sanding sugar inside the cookie cutter until the glaze is covered. Carefully lift off the cookie cutter. Decorate the remaining cupcakes in the same way, then let them dry until the glaze is set, about 30 minutes.

Fruity Cupcakes

★

Piña Colada Cupcakes

The combination of pineapple and coconut is terrifically tropical. Pineapple juice and crushed pineapple in the batter make these cupcakes very moist, and adding coconut extract to the tangy cream cheese frosting is the secret to their irresistible flavor.

MAKES 16 CUPCAKES

1½ cups all-purpose flour

1 cup sweetened shredded coconut, toasted (see page 21)

1¼ teaspoons baking powder

¼ teaspoon salt

1 (8-ounce) can crushed pineapple, drained, juice reserved

½ cup canned coconut milk

¾ cup plus 2 tablespoons sugar

½ cup (1 stick) unsalted butter, at room temperature

1 large egg plus 1 large egg white

1 teaspoon vanilla extract

Coconut–Cream Cheese Frosting (page 108)

Pastel-colored sprinkles, for decorating (optional)

 Preheat the oven to 350°F. Line 16 cups of two standard 12-cup muffin pans with paper or foil liners.

In a medium bowl, whisk together the flour, toasted coconut, baking powder, and salt. In a liquid measuring cup, stir together ½ cup of the reserved pineapple juice and the coconut milk. In a large bowl, using an electric mixer, beat the sugar and butter on medium-high speed until light and fluffy, 2 to 3 minutes. Add the egg, egg white, and vanilla and beat until combined. Turn off the mixer and scrape down the bowl with a rubber spatula. Add about one-third of the flour mixture and mix on low speed just until blended. Pour in about half of the coconut milk mixture and mix on low speed just until combined. Add about half of the remaining flour mixture and mix on low speed just until blended. Pour in the remaining coconut milk mixture and mix just until combined. Add the remaining flour mixture and mix just until blended. Turn off the mixer, scrape down the bowl, and stir in ½ cup of the crushed pineapple with the spatula. (Reserve the remaining pineapple for another use.)

Divide the batter evenly among the prepared muffin cups. Bake until the tops are light golden brown and a toothpick inserted into the center of a cupcake comes out clean, 18 to 20 minutes. Remove the pans from the oven and set them on a wire rack. Let cool for 10 minutes, then carefully transfer the cupcakes directly to the rack. Let cool completely, about 1 hour.

Using a pastry bag fitted with a large plain tip (see page 15; we used Ateco 809), top the cupcakes with the frosting and decorate with sprinkles (if using).

Triple Berry Cupcakes

Raspberry jam is baked into the center of vanilla cupcakes, adding a fun burst of color and flavor. Make these cupcakes at the height of summer, when berries are at their sweetest. Once they are decorated, serve them right away, while the berries are fresh.

MAKES 12 CUPCAKES

Vanilla Cupcakes (page 36), prepared through step 2

¼ cup raspberry jam or preserves

Cream Cheese Frosting (page 108)

3 cups mixed fresh berries, such as raspberries, blackberries, blueberries, and/or strawberries

Fresh mint leaves, for serving (optional)

Divide the cupcake batter evenly among the prepared muffin cups. Drop 1 teaspoon raspberry jam onto the center of each (the jam will sink into the batter during baking). Bake until the tops are light golden brown and a toothpick inserted into the center of a cupcake comes out with only a few crumbs and raspberry jam attached, 18 to 20 minutes. Remove the pan from the oven and set it on a wire rack. Let cool for 10 minutes, then transfer the cupcakes directly to the rack. Let cool completely, about 1 hour.

Using a small icing spatula or a butter knife, or a pastry bag fitted with a large plain tip (see page 15), top the cupcakes with the frosting, then decorate with an assortment of berries, dividing them evenly, and mint leaves (if using).

Berries and Cream

Fresh, seasonal berries are also the perfect partner for a light-as-air whipped cream frosting. Try these fruity cupcakes topped with swirls of Sweetened Whipped Cream (page 107) instead of the Cream Cheese Frosting, but be sure to store them in the refrigerator if you aren't eating them right away.

Apple Crumb Cupcakes

Large chunks of apple give these cupcakes a rustic, hearty texture. Use either tart apples like Granny Smith or sweet ones such as Fuji. Just make sure the apples have a crisp, firm texture. The buttery topping turns deliciously crunchy during baking.

MAKES 12 CUPCAKES

2 tablespoons plus 6 tablespoons (¾ stick) unsalted butter, at room temperature

1 pound crisp apples, peeled, cored, and cut into 1-inch chunks

2 tablespoons plus ¾ cup sugar

1 cup all-purpose flour

¾ teaspoon baking powder

½ teaspoon salt

¼ teaspoon baking soda

½ teaspoon ground cinnamon

¼ teaspoon ground allspice

Pinch of ground nutmeg

2 large eggs

½ teaspoon vanilla extract

¼ cup sour cream

Crumb Topping (page 119)

 Preheat the oven to 350°F. Line a standard 12-cup muffin pan with paper or foil liners.

In a medium saucepan over medium-high heat, melt the 2 tablespoons butter. Add the apple chunks and the 2 tablespoons sugar and cook, stirring often, until the apples are tender and soft, 5 to 7 minutes. Transfer the mixture to a bowl and let cool completely.

In a medium bowl, whisk together the flour, baking powder, salt, baking soda, cinnamon, allspice, and nutmeg. In a large bowl, using an electric mixer, beat the 6 tablespoons butter and the ¾ cup sugar on medium-high speed until light and fluffy, 2 to 3 minutes. Add the eggs one at a time, beating well after each addition. Add the vanilla and beat until combined. Add about half of the flour mixture and mix on low speed just until blended. Add the sour cream and mix on low speed until combined. Add the remaining flour mixture and mix just until blended. Turn off the mixer, add the apples, and mix with a spatula until well combined.

Divide the batter evenly among the prepared muffin cups. Sprinkle with the crumb topping, dividing it evenly. Bake until the topping is golden brown and a toothpick inserted into the center of a cupcake comes out clean, 18 to 20 minutes. Remove the pan from the oven and set it on a wire rack. Let cool for 5 minutes, then carefully transfer the cupcakes directly to the rack. Let cool completely, about 1 hour.

Lemon-Blueberry Crunch Cupcakes

The "crunch" in these crazy-good cupcakes comes from the sugar sprinkled onto the fresh blueberries placed on top of the batter just before baking. A drizzle of lemon glaze adds sweet-tart, lip-puckering flavor.

MAKES 12 CUPCAKES

1¼ cups all-purpose flour

½ teaspoon baking powder

½ teaspoon baking soda

¼ teaspoon salt

¾ cup sugar, plus
2 tablespoons for topping

4 tablespoons (½ stick)
unsalted butter,
at room temperature

1 large egg

2 teaspoons finely
grated lemon zest

¾ cup sour cream

1¼ cups fresh blueberries

Lemon Glaze (page 114)

 Preheat the oven to 350°F. Line a standard 12-cup muffin pan with paper or foil liners.

In a medium bowl, whisk together the flour, baking powder, baking soda, and salt. In a large bowl, using an electric mixer, beat the ¾ cup sugar and the butter on medium-high speed until light and fluffy, 2 to 3 minutes. Add the egg and lemon zest and beat until combined. Turn off the mixer and scrape down the bowl with a rubber spatula. Add about half of the flour mixture and mix on low speed just until blended. Add the sour cream and mix on low speed until combined. Add the remaining flour mixture and mix just until blended. Turn off the mixer, scrape down the bowl, and give the batter a final stir with the spatula.

Divide the batter evenly among the prepared muffin cups. Arrange the blueberries in a single layer on top of the batter, dividing them evenly, then sprinkle with the remaining 2 tablespoons sugar, dividing it evenly. Bake until the blueberries burst and a toothpick inserted into the center of a cupcake comes out clean, 18 to 20 minutes. Remove the pan from the oven and set it on a wire rack. Let cool for 10 minutes, then carefully transfer the cupcakes directly to the rack. Let cool completely, about 1 hour.

Use a spoon to drizzle the cupcakes with the glaze.

Orange-Vanilla Swirl Cupcakes

We took the flavors of a favorite frozen treat and baked them into a cupcake! To create a pretty two-tone swirl, divide the frosting in half, tint one portion orange, then put both colors in the same pastry bag, placing orange frosting on one side and white on the other.

MAKES 12 CUPCAKES

1¼ cups all-purpose flour

1¼ teaspoons
baking powder

¼ teaspoon salt

¾ cup sugar

6 tablespoons (¾ stick)
unsalted butter,
at room temperature

2 large eggs

1 teaspoon vanilla extract

1 teaspoon grated
orange zest

½ cup fresh orange juice

Cream Cheese Frosting
(page 108)

Red gel paste
food coloring

Yellow gel paste
food coloring

 Preheat the oven to 350°F. Line a standard 12-cup muffin pan with paper or foil liners.

In a medium bowl, whisk together the flour, baking powder, and salt. In a large bowl, using an electric mixer, beat the sugar and butter on medium-high speed until light and fluffy, 2 to 3 minutes. Add the eggs, vanilla, and orange zest and beat until combined. Add half of the flour mixture and mix on low speed just until blended. Pour in the orange juice and mix on low speed just until combined. Add the remaining flour mixture and mix on low speed just until blended. Turn off the mixer, scrape down the bowl, and give the batter a final stir with the spatula.

Divide the batter evenly among the prepared muffin cups. Bake until the tops are light golden brown and a toothpick inserted into the center of a cupcake comes out clean, 18 to 20 minutes. Remove the pan from the oven and set it on a wire rack. Let cool for 10 minutes, then carefully transfer the cupcakes directly to the rack. Let cool completely, about 1 hour.

Divide the frosting between two small bowls. Add 1 dab of red food coloring and 2 dabs of yellow food coloring to one bowl, then mix with a rubber spatula until the frosting is tinted orange. Fit a pastry bag with a star tip (see page 15; we used Ateco 826). Transfer the orange frosting to the pastry bag, keeping it on one side; transfer the white frosting to the other side of the pastry bag. Pipe the frosting onto the cupcakes.

Banana Split Cupcakes

These giant sundae-inspired cupcakes have a lot of layers, but they're easy to assemble once you have the cupcakes made and the toppings ready to go. A scoop of strawberry frosting stands in for ice cream, and chocolate glaze takes the place of hot fudge.

MAKES 18 CUPCAKES

Strawberry–Cream Cheese Frosting (page 108)

Banana Cupcakes (page 31), baked and cooled

Rich Chocolate Glaze (page 114)

Sweetened Whipped Cream (page 107)

Dried banana chips or sprinkles, for decorating (optional)

 Use an ice cream scoop to place a large ball of frosting onto each cupcake so that the frosting looks like a scoop of ice cream.

Using a spoon, drizzle the chocolate glaze on top of the frosting, letting the glaze run down the sides a little. Let the glaze set for about 5 minutes.

Fit a pastry bag with a star tip (see page 15), then transfer the whipped cream to the bag. Pipe whipped cream on top of each cupcake. Decorate with dried banana chips or sprinkles (if using).

Mini Strawberry Cheesecake Cupcakes

These little delights are tiny three-bite versions of classic New York cheesecake. They combine sweet, fresh strawberries with the rich creaminess of cheesecake, and they taste every bit as awesome as a full-sized version.

MAKES 24 MINI CUPCAKES

CUPCAKES

2¼ (8-ounce) packages cream cheese, at room temperature

¾ cup sugar

¼ cup sour cream

½ teaspoon vanilla extract

2 large eggs

3 tablespoons all-purpose flour

TOPPING

1 pound fresh strawberries, hulled and cut in half

½ cup plus 2 tablespoons sugar

1 tablespoon fresh lemon juice

Preheat the oven to 350°F. Line a 24-cup mini muffin pan with foil liners.

To make the cupcakes, in a large bowl, using an electric mixer, beat the cream cheese on medium-high speed until fluffy, about 3 minutes. With the mixer running on low speed, gradually add the sugar and beat until smooth. Turn off the mixer and scrape down the sides of the bowl with a rubber spatula. Add the sour cream and vanilla and beat on medium speed until combined. Add the eggs one at a time, beating well after each addition. Add the flour and beat on low speed until combined.

Divide the cream cheese filling evenly among the prepared muffin cups. Bake until the cupcakes are just set in the center, about 15 minutes. Remove the pan from the oven and set it on a wire rack. Let the cupcakes cool in the pan for 5 minutes, then transfer them directly to the wire rack to cool completely, about 45 minutes. Refrigerate the cupcakes, stacked between sheets of parchment paper, in an airtight container, for at least 12 hours or up to 3 days.

To make the topping, in a medium saucepan, combine half of the strawberries and all of the sugar. Using a fork, gently mash the strawberries into small pieces. Set the pan over medium-high heat and cook, stirring occasionally, until the strawberries are softened, about 3 minutes. Remove from the heat and stir in the remaining strawberries and the lemon juice. Transfer to a small bowl, let cool completely, then cover and refrigerate until ready to serve. To serve, spoon about 1 tablespoon of the topping onto each chilled cupcake.

Blackberry-Coconut Cupcakes

Blackberry jam adds pretty color as well as yummy flavor to cream cheese frosting. Baked in purple liners and decorated with purple sprinkles and silver stars, these cosmic cupcakes will make you think of a star-filled nighttime sky.

MAKES 12 CUPCAKES

1 cup all-purpose flour

½ cup sweetened shredded coconut, roughly chopped

1¼ teaspoons baking powder

¼ teaspoon salt

¾ cup plus 2 tablespoons sugar

½ cup (1 stick) unsalted butter, at room temperature

1 large egg plus 1 large egg white

1 teaspoon vanilla extract

½ cup canned coconut milk

Blackberry–Cream Cheese Frosting (page 108)

Purple sprinkles and/ or edible silver stars, for decorating (optional)

Preheat the oven to 350°F. Line a standard 12-cup muffin pan with paper or foil liners.

In a medium bowl, whisk together the flour, coconut, baking powder, and salt. In a large bowl, using an electric mixer, beat the sugar and butter on medium-high speed until light and fluffy, 2 to 3 minutes. Add the egg, egg white, and vanilla and beat until combined. Turn off the mixer and scrape down the bowl with a rubber spatula. Add half of the flour mixture and mix on low speed just until blended. Pour in the coconut milk and mix on low speed just until combined. Add the remaining flour mixture and mix on low speed just until blended. Turn off the mixer, scrape down the bowl, and give the batter a final stir with the spatula.

Divide the batter evenly among the prepared muffin cups. Bake until the tops are light golden brown and a toothpick inserted into the center of a cupcake comes out clean, 18 to 20 minutes. Remove the pan from the oven and set it on a wire rack. Let cool for 10 minutes, then carefully transfer the cupcakes directly to the rack. Let cool completely, about 1 hour.

Using a small icing spatula or a butter knife, or a pastry bag fitted with a large star tip (see page 15; we used Ateco 849), top the cupcakes with the frosting and decorate with sprinkles and/or stars (if using).

Chocolate Cupcakes

Cookie-tastic
For an extra-crunchy cupcake, sprinkle big chunks of crushed cookies on top of the cookie frosting.

Cookies 'n' Cream Cupcakes

Have you ever had a cookie in your cupcake? A chocolate sandwich cookie hides at the bottom of each of these sweet treats, and crushed cookies add crunchy bites to the vanilla frosting for the ultimate cookies 'n' cream dream.

MAKES 16 CUPCAKES

24 chocolate-creme
sandwich cookies

Devil's Food Cupcakes
(page 18), prepared
through step 2; omit
the chocolate glaze and
sugared flowers

Fluffy Vanilla Frosting
(page 104)

Preheat the oven to 350°F. Line 16 cups of two standard muffin pans with paper or foil liners. Place 1 cookie in the bottom of each cup.

Divide the cupcake batter evenly among the muffin cups. Bake until a toothpick inserted into the center of a cupcake comes out clean, 18 to 20 minutes. Remove the pans from the oven and set them on a wire rack. Let cool for 10 minutes, then carefully transfer the cupcakes directly to the rack. Let cool completely, about 1 hour.

Place the remaining 8 cookies in a zipper-lock bag, seal the bag, and use a rolling pin or wooden spoon to crush the cookies to small pieces.

Place the frosting in a medium bowl, then add the cookie pieces. Beat on medium speed until well combined and the cookies are broken into coarse crumbs. If you will be piping the frosting onto the cupcakes, the cookie crumbs need to be fine enough to pass through the pastry tip.

Using a small icing spatula or a butter knife, or a pastry bag fitted with a plain tip (see page 15), top the cupcakes with the frosting.

Mini Chocolate-Mint Cupcakes

These tiny cupcakes have a fudgy brownie-like texture. They're flavored inside and out with cool, refreshing peppermint. Fresh bright-green mint leaves make pretty decorations, but you could also dust the cupcakes with green sanding sugar or sprinkles.

MAKES 24 MINI CUPCAKES

4 ounces bittersweet chocolate, chopped

4 tablespoons (½ stick) unsalted butter, cut into chunks

¾ cup sugar

2 large eggs

½ teaspoon vanilla extract

¼ teaspoon peppermint extract

¼ teaspoon salt

¼ cup plus 2 tablespoons all-purpose flour

Fluffy Mint Frosting (page 104)

Small fresh mint leaves, for decorating (optional)

 Preheat the oven to 350°F. Line a 24-cup mini muffin pan with paper or foil liners.

In a medium microwave-safe bowl, combine the chocolate and butter. Microwave on high power, stirring every 20 seconds, just until the mixture is melted and smooth. Let cool completely.

Add the sugar to the chocolate mixture and stir with a whisk until blended. Whisk in the eggs one at a time, mixing until well combined after each addition. Whisk in the vanilla, peppermint extract, and salt. Add the flour and fold gently with a rubber spatula just until no white streaks remain; do not overmix.

Divide the batter evenly among the prepared muffin cups. Bake until the tops are crackly and a toothpick inserted into the center of a cupcake comes out with only a few crumbs attached, 18 to 20 minutes. Remove the pan from the oven and set it on a wire rack. Let cool for 10 minutes, then carefully transfer the cupcakes directly to the rack. Let cool completely, about 1 hour.

Using a small icing spatula or a butter knife, or a pastry bag fitted with a star tip (see page 15; we used Ateco 826), top the cupcakes with the frosting, then decorate with mint leaves (if using).

Chocolate-Peanut Butter Cupcakes

Who doesn't love the classic candy bar combination of chocolate and peanut butter? To adapt those yummy flavors into a cupcake, top a dark chocolate base with fluffy peanut butter frosting and sprinkle a bunch of chocolate–peanut butter candies on top.

MAKES 12 CUPCAKES

Devil's Food Cupcakes (page 18), baked and cooled; omit the chocolate glaze and sugared flowers

Peanut Butter Frosting (page 111)

Chocolate–peanut butter candies, such as peanut butter M&M's, Reese's Pieces, or chopped peanut butter cups, for decorating (optional)

Using a small icing spatula or a butter knife, or a pastry bag fitted with a plain or star tip (see page 15), top the cupcakes with the frosting, then decorate with chocolate–peanut butter candies (if using).

Frosting Fun!

Chocolate cupcakes can be paired with so many different frostings. Fluffy White Chocolate Frosting (page 104), Fluffy Coconut Frosting (page 104), or even Strawberry–Cream Cheese Frosting (page 108) would all be delicious, or create your own unique combination. Then select candies or decorations that match your flavor theme.

Triple Chocolate Cupcakes

Milk chocolate cupcakes filled with gooey dark chocolate and topped with white chocolate frosting are a chocolate lover's dream. To warm the glaze filling, heat it in a bowl set over, but not touching, a saucepan of simmering water until it is spoonable.

MAKES 12 CUPCAKES

½ cup (1 stick) plus
3 tablespoons unsalted
butter, cut into chunks

3 ounces milk chocolate,
chopped

⅔ cup all-purpose flour

2½ tablespoons
unsweetened
cocoa powder

¾ teaspoon baking powder

¼ teaspoon salt

¾ cup sugar

3 large eggs

1 teaspoon vanilla extract

¾ cup Rich Chocolate
Glaze (page 114), warm

Fluffy White Chocolate
Frosting (page 104)

 Preheat the oven to 350°F. Line a standard 12-cup muffin pan with paper or foil liners.

In a large microwave-safe bowl, combine the butter and chocolate. Microwave on high power, stirring every 20 seconds, just until the mixture is melted and smooth. Don't let it get too hot! Let cool completely.

In a medium bowl, whisk together the flour, cocoa powder, baking powder, and salt. Add the sugar to the chocolate mixture and whisk until blended. Whisk in the eggs one at a time, mixing until well combined after each addition. Whisk in the vanilla. Add the flour mixture and fold gently with a rubber spatula.

Divide the batter evenly among the prepared muffin cups. Bake until a toothpick inserted into the center of a cupcake comes out with only a few crumbs attached, 22 to 24 minutes. Remove the pan from the oven and set it on a wire rack. Let cool for 10 minutes, then carefully transfer the cupcakes directly to the rack. Let cool completely, about 1 hour.

Using a paring knife, cut a 1½-inch-diameter round about 1 inch deep in the center of each cupcake, then remove the rounds (and enjoy them as a baker's treat). Fill each hollow with about 1 tablespoon of the chocolate glaze. Place the filled cupcakes on a rimmed cookie sheet and refrigerate until the filling is set, about 10 minutes.

Using a small icing spatula or a butter knife, frost the cupcakes.

Hot Chocolate Cupcakes

Nothing's better on a cold winter's day than a cup of hot chocolate topped with tons of marshmallows. These chocolaty glazed cupcakes capture all that yumminess, with a marshmallow creme filling inside and a pile of mini marshmallows on top.

MAKES 12 CUPCAKES

Devil's Food Cupcakes (page 18), prepared through step 2; omit the sugared flowers

FILLING

¾ cup powdered sugar

3 tablespoons unsalted butter, at room temperature

½ cup marshmallow creme

1 tablespoon heavy cream

½ teaspoon vanilla extract

Rich Chocolate Glaze (page 114)

Mini marshmallows, for decorating

Unsweetened cocoa powder, for decorating (optional)

Divide the batter evenly among the prepared muffin cups. Bake until a toothpick inserted into the center of a cupcake comes out clean, 18 to 20 minutes. Remove the pan from the oven and set it on a wire rack. Let cool for 10 minutes, then carefully transfer the cupcakes directly to the rack. Let cool completely, about 1 hour.

To make the filling, in a medium bowl, combine the powdered sugar and butter. Using an electric mixer, beat on medium speed until lightened, about 3 minutes. Turn off the mixer and scrape down the bowl with a rubber spatula. Add the marshmallow creme, heavy cream, and vanilla and beat on medium speed until light and fluffy, about 3 minutes.

Using a paring knife, cut a 1½-inch-diameter round about 1 inch deep in the center of each cupcake, then remove the rounds (and enjoy them as a baker's treat). Fill each hollow with a spoonful of the filling.

Spoon the glaze over the filled cupcakes. Top with mini marshmallows, then dust lightly with cocoa powder (if using).

White Chocolate-Raspberry Cupcakes

Sweet white chocolate and fresh raspberries are always a great combination, and their colors look pretty together, too. Choose good-quality white chocolate that comes in a bar or block for this recipe; don't use white chocolate chips because they don't melt well.

MAKES 12 CUPCAKES

2 ounces white chocolate, chopped, plus an extra chunk, for decorating

2 cups all-purpose flour

2 teaspoons baking powder

¼ teaspoon salt

½ cup (1 stick) unsalted butter, at room temperature

1 cup sugar

3 large egg whites

½ cup whole milk

1 (6-ounce) container fresh raspberries

Fluffy Raspberry Frosting (page 104)

 Preheat the oven to 350°F. Line a standard 12-cup muffin pan with paper or foil liners.

Place the white chocolate in a small microwave-safe bowl. Microwave on high power, stirring every 20 seconds, just until the chocolate is melted and smooth. Set the chocolate aside.

In a large bowl, whisk together the flour, baking powder, and salt. Using an electric mixer, beat the butter and sugar on medium-high speed until light and fluffy, 2 to 3 minutes. Add the egg whites and beat until combined. Add half of the flour mixture and mix on low speed just until blended. Pour in the milk and mix on low speed just until combined. Add the remaining flour mixture and mix on low speed just until blended. Add the white chocolate and stir with a spatula just until blended, then gently fold in the raspberries.

Divide the batter evenly among the prepared muffin cups. Bake until the cupcakes are light golden brown and a toothpick inserted into the center of a cupcake comes out clean, about 25 minutes. Remove the pan from the oven and set it on a wire rack. Let cool for 10 minutes, then carefully transfer the cupcakes directly to the rack. Let cool completely, about 1 hour.

Using a small icing spatula or a butter knife, or a pastry bag fitted with a star tip (see page 15; we used Ateco 826), top the cupcakes with the frosting. Use a vegetable peeler to shave long curls from the chunk of white chocolate and place the curls on top of the frosting.

Rocky Road Cupcakes

Chocolate, nuts, and marshmallows are the tasty trio that make up rocky road. These cupcakes have walnuts baked in and on top, but you can use just about any type of nut in their place—or skip the nuts altogether, if you like.

MAKES 12 CUPCAKES

2 cups walnut halves, toasted and roughly chopped

Chocolate Cupcakes (page 25), prepared through step 4; omit the vanilla frosting and food coloring

Marshmallow Frosting (page 110)

Add 1½ cups of the walnuts to the cupcake batter and stir just until combined. Divide the batter evenly among the prepared muffin cups. Sprinkle the remaining ½ cup walnuts on top of the batter in each cup, dividing it evenly. Bake until a toothpick inserted into the center of a cupcake comes out with only a few crumbs attached, 22 to 24 minutes. Remove the pan from the oven and set it on a wire rack. Let cool for 10 minutes, then carefully transfer the cupcakes directly to the rack. Let cool completely, about 1 hour.

Using a small icing spatula or a butter knife, or a pastry bag fitted with a plain or star tip (see page 15), top the cupcakes with the frosting.

Molten Chocolate Cupcakes

These cupcakes bake up as light as air but with a tasty surprise: gooey dark-chocolate centers. A mound of Sweetened Whipped Cream (page 107) or scoop of vanilla ice cream is the perfect partner for these deliciously warm and very elegant little cakes.

MAKES 12 CUPCAKES

4 ounces semisweet chocolate, chopped

4 tablespoons (½ stick) unsalted butter, cut into chunks

3 large eggs, separated

2 tablespoons all-purpose flour

Pinch of salt

¼ cup sugar

4 ounces bittersweet chocolate, broken into 12 even pieces

Sweetened Whipped Cream (page 107) or vanilla ice cream, for serving

 Preheat the oven to 375°F. Lightly spray a standard 12-cup muffin pan with nonstick cooking spray.

In a large microwave-safe bowl, combine the chocolate and butter. Microwave on high power, stirring every 20 seconds, just until the mixture is melted and smooth. Don't let it get too hot! Let cool slightly.

Add the egg yolks to the chocolate mixture and whisk until well combined. Add the flour and whisk until combined.

In a clean medium bowl, using an electric mixer with clean attachments, beat the egg whites and salt on medium-high speed until foamy, about 4 minutes. While beating, gradually add the sugar, then continue to beat until the egg whites hold soft peaks when the beaters are lifted. Using a rubber spatula, gently fold one-third of the beaten egg whites into the chocolate mixture to lighten it. Fold in the remaining beaten egg whites in 2 additions just until no white streaks remain.

Divide the batter evenly among the prepared muffin cups. Bake for 5 minutes, then remove the pan from the oven and set it on a wire rack. Working quickly, insert 1 piece of bittersweet chocolate into the center of each cupcake. Return the pan to the oven and continue to bake until the cupcakes are well-risen and brown around the edges, 3 to 5 minutes more. Remove the pan from the oven and set it on the rack. Let cool for 5 minutes, then use a small offset spatula to transfer the cupcakes to plates. Dollop with whipped cream and serve warm.

Specialty Cupcakes

Piñata Cupcakes

With these fun, festive cupcakes, your friends are in for a surprise! One bite reveals a big pile of sprinkles hiding inside. The frosting is tinted with pink and blue swirls, but you can use your favorite colors, or match them to the theme of your party.

MAKES 12 CUPCAKES

Vanilla Cupcakes (page 36), baked and cooled

Fluffy Vanilla Frosting (page 104)

½ cup star-shaped or other shaped sprinkles

Blue gel paste food coloring

Pink gel paste food coloring

Using a paring knife, cut a 1½-inch-diameter round about 1 inch deep in the center of each cupcake, then remove the rounds and set them aside. Fill each hollow with about 2 teaspoons of sprinkles. Cut the rounds that you removed from the cupcakes in half horizontally; reserve the tops and discard—or eat!—the rest. Return the tops to the cupcakes, covering the sprinkles, then gently press down on each to fit it into the hole.

Fit a large pastry bag with a large star tip (see page 15; we used Ateco 826). Using a paintbrush, paint a stripe of blue food coloring from tip to top against the side of the pastry bag, then paint another blue stripe against the other side of the bag, opposite the first stripe. Clean the brush and paint a stripe of pink food coloring against the side of the pastry bag between the blue stripes, then paint a second pink stripe opposite the first pink stripe. Carefully transfer the frosting to the pastry bag; try not to disturb the stripes. Pipe the frosting onto the cupcakes.

Watermelon Cupcakes

Even though there isn't any watermelon flavoring in these cupcakes, the green base, pink frosting, and mini chocolate chips that look like seeds make for super-cute treats that are perfect for a summer cookout.

MAKES 12 CUPCAKES

Green gel paste food coloring

Vanilla Cupcakes (page 36), prepared through step 2

Pink gel paste food coloring

Fluffy Vanilla Frosting (page 104)

Mini semisweet chocolate chips, for decorating

 Add 1 dab of green food coloring to the cupcake batter and mix until the batter is evenly tinted; it should be lime green in color.

Divide the batter evenly among the prepared muffin cups. Bake until the tops are light golden brown and a toothpick inserted into the center of a cupcake comes out clean, 18 to 20 minutes. Remove the pan from the oven and set it on a wire rack. Let cool for 10 minutes, then carefully transfer the cupcakes directly to the rack. Let cool completely, about 1 hour.

Add 2 dabs of pink food coloring to the frosting. Using a rubber spatula, mix until the frosting is evenly tinted; it should be bright pink. Fit a large pastry bag with a star tip (see page 15; we used Ateco 826), then transfer the frosting to the bag. Pipe the frosting on the cupcakes and sprinkle the top with mini chocolate chips.

Birthday Cake Cupcakes

With festive, colorful sprinkles in the cupcakes as well as on top of them, these are the perfect treats for birthday celebrations. If you like, swap Fluffy Vanilla Frosting (page 104) for the chocolate frosting, or use sprinkles that match the party's color scheme.

MAKES 24 CUPCAKES

2 tablespoons rainbow sprinkles, plus more for decorating

Yellow Cupcakes (page 27), prepared through step 2

Chocolate Frosting (page 113)

 Add the sprinkles to the cupcake batter and use a rubber spatula to carefully fold them into the batter until just combined.

Divide the batter evenly among the prepared muffin cups. Bake until the tops are light golden brown and a toothpick inserted into the center of a cupcake comes out clean, about 17 minutes. Remove the pan from the oven and set it on a wire rack. Let cool for 10 minutes, then carefully transfer the cupcakes directly to the rack. Let cool completely, about 1 hour.

Using a small icing spatula or a butter knife, or a pastry bag fitted with a star tip (see page 15; we used Ateco 826), top the cupcakes with the frosting, then decorate with sprinkles.

Salted Caramel Cupcakes

Salt really enhances the flavor of caramel, making it taste richer and more mouthwatering. For an extra-special touch, you can decorate the cupcakes with caramel candies and place them on top of the caramel-swirled frosting.

MAKES 12 CUPCAKES

1¼ cups all-purpose flour

¾ teaspoon baking powder

¼ teaspoon salt

1 cup firmly packed dark brown sugar

½ cup granulated sugar

½ cup (1 stick) unsalted butter, at room temperature

2 large eggs

1 teaspoon vanilla extract

½ cup whole milk

Caramel Drizzle (page 118)

Fluffy Vanilla Frosting (page 104)

12 caramel candies (optional)

Sea salt

Preheat the oven to 350°F. Line a standard 12-cup muffin pan with paper or foil liners.

In a medium bowl, whisk together the flour, baking powder, and salt. In a large bowl, using an electric mixer, beat the brown sugar, granulated sugar, and butter on medium-high speed until light and fluffy, 2 to 3 minutes. Add the eggs one at a time, beating well after each addition. Turn off the mixer and scrape down the bowl with a rubber spatula. Add the vanilla and beat until combined. Turn off the mixer. Add half of the flour mixture and mix on low speed just until blended. Pour in the milk and mix on low speed just until combined. Add the remaining flour mixture and mix on low speed just until blended. Turn off the mixer and scrape down the bowl.

Divide the batter evenly among the prepared muffin cups. Bake until a toothpick inserted into the center of a cupcake comes out clean, 20 to 22 minutes. Remove the pan from the oven and set it on a wire rack. Let cool for 10 minutes, then carefully transfer the cupcakes directly to the rack. Let cool completely, about 1 hour.

Add the caramel drizzle to the frosting and, with a butter knife, carefully swirl it in so that streaks of caramel are still visible. Using a small icing spatula or a butter knife, or a pastry bag fitted with a plain or star tip (see page 15), top the cupcakes with the frosting. Decorate each cupcake with a caramel candy (if using) and sprinkle with a pinch of sea salt.

Mini Cookie Dough Cupcakes

Gooey and chewy, these tiny treats taste like two-bite nuggets of buttery chocolate chip cookie dough. They're delicious on their own, but if you can't get enough chocolate, top each with a dollop of Chocolate Frosting (page 113) or Rich Chocolate Glaze (page 114).

MAKES 32 MINI CUPCAKES

1½ cups all-purpose flour

1¼ teaspoons baking powder

¼ teaspoon salt

6 tablespoons (¾ stick) unsalted butter, at room temperature

1¼ cups firmly packed light brown sugar

2 large eggs

1 teaspoon vanilla extract

1 cup mini semisweet chocolate chips

 Preheat the oven to 350°F. Line a 24-cup mini muffin pan with paper or foil liners.

In a medium bowl, whisk together the flour, baking powder, and salt. In a large bowl, using an electric mixer, beat the butter and brown sugar on medium speed until light and fluffy, 3 to 5 minutes. Add the eggs one at a time, beating well after each addition. Add the vanilla and beat until well combined. Turn off the mixer and scrape down the bowl with a rubber spatula. Add the flour mixture and mix on low speed just until blended. Turn off the mixer, add the chocolate chips, and stir with a rubber spatula until the chips are mixed evenly into the batter.

Spoon 1 tablespoon of batter into each cup of the prepared muffin tin. Bake until the tops start to turn light golden brown, 14 to 16 minutes. Remove the pan from the oven and set it on a wire rack. Let cool for about 10 minutes, then carefully transfer the cupcakes directly to the rack. Let cool completely.

Line 8 cups of the same muffin pan with paper or foil liners. Portion and bake the remaining batter in the same way.

Baker's tip
Freezing the first layer of frosting for a few minutes will help the layer of chocolate glaze set quickly without running.

Sundae Cupcakes

Are they ice cream sundaes? Or are they cupcakes? These adorable little treats will make you do a double take! Vanilla frosting masquerades as the ice cream and whipped cream, and chocolate glaze, colorful sprinkles, and maraschino cherries finish off the look.

MAKES 12 CUPCAKES

Double recipe Fluffy Vanilla Frosting (page 104)

Vanilla Cupcakes (page 36), baked and cooled

Rich Chocolate Glaze (page 114), warm

Rainbow nonpareil sprinkles (about ½ cup)

12 maraschino cherries

Fit a pastry bag with a large round tip (see page 15; we used Ateco 809) and fill it with one batch of the frosting. Pipe frosting on a cupcake in a thick, even layer, starting from the outer edge and spiraling toward the center. Repeat with the remaining cupcakes, then place them on a rimmed cookie sheet and freeze them for 20 minutes to firm up the frosting.

Place the warm chocolate glaze in a medium bowl and pour the sprinkles onto a small plate. One at a time, dip just the frosted part of each chilled cupcake into the glaze, then into the sprinkles. Return the cupcakes to the cookie sheet and freeze for 5 minutes to firm up the glaze.

Fit another pastry bag with a large star tip (we used Ateco 826) and fill it with the second batch of frosting. Pipe the frosting on top of the cupcakes, dividing it evenly, and top each with a maraschino cherry.

Cupcake Cones

It's surprisingly simple to create these faux ice cream cones! Just fill wafer cones with cupcake batter, then bake them in a standard muffin pan. You can vary the batter, frosting, and sprinkles to create different looks and flavor combos.

MAKES 12 CUPCAKE CONES

12 jumbo flat-bottomed wafer ice cream cones

Vanilla Cupcakes (page 36), prepared through step 2

Double recipe Fluffy Vanilla Frosting (page 104)

Rich Chocolate Glaze (page 114), warm

Rainbow nonpareil sprinkles (about ½ cup)

12 maraschino cherries

Place an ice cream cone in each cup of a standard 12-cup muffin pan. Divide the batter evenly among the cones, filling each about two-thirds full. Bake until the tops are light golden brown and a toothpick inserted into the center of a cupcake comes out clean, 18 to 20 minutes. Remove the pan from the oven and set it on a wire rack. Let cool for 10 minutes, then carefully transfer the cones directly to the rack. Let cool completely, about 1 hour.

Fit a pastry bag with a large round tip (see page 15; we used Ateco 809) and fill it with one batch of the frosting. Pipe frosting on a cupcake in a thick, even layer, starting from the outer edge and spiraling toward the center. Repeat with the remaining cupcakes, then place them on a rimmed cookie sheet and freeze them for 20 minutes to firm up the frosting.

Place the warm chocolate glaze in a medium bowl and pour the sprinkles onto a small plate. One at a time, dip just the frosted part of each chilled cupcake into the glaze, then into the sprinkles. Return the cupcake cones to the cookie sheet and freeze for 5 minutes to firm up the glaze.

Fit another pastry bag with a large star tip (we used Ateco 826) and fill it with the second batch of frosting. Pipe the frosting on top of the cupcake cones, dividing it evenly, and top each with a maraschino cherry.

Sprinkle Cupcakes

Tailor these colorful cupcakes to match your party theme. For the Fourth of July, use red, white, and blue sprinkles, then divide the frosting into thirds and tint one portion red and another blue. Or use pink and red sprinkles and frosting for Valentine's Day.

MAKES 12 CUPCAKES

2 tablespoons rainbow nonpareil sprinkles

Vanilla Cupcakes (page 36), prepared through step 2

Turquoise gel paste food coloring

Fluffy Vanilla Frosting (page 104)

Pastel or rainbow confetti sprinkles, for decorating

 Add the nonpareil sprinkles to the cupcake batter and use a rubber spatula to carefully fold them into the batter until just combined.

Divide the batter evenly among the prepared muffin cups. Bake until the tops are light golden brown and a toothpick inserted into the center of a cupcake comes out clean, 18 to 20 minutes. Remove the pan from the oven and set it on a wire rack. Let cool for 10 minutes, then carefully transfer the cupcakes directly to the rack. Let cool completely, about 1 hour.

Add 2 dabs of food coloring to the frosting. Using a rubber spatula, mix until the frosting is evenly tinted. Using a small icing spatula or a butter knife, or a pastry bag fitted with a plain tip (see page 15), top the cupcakes with the frosting, then decorate them with confetti sprinkles.

Brown Butter & Honey Cupcakes

When butter is cooked until it turns golden brown, it smells like toasted nuts and is delicious. These treats are decorated to look like beehives, and the frosting tastes of honey. Bees made from marzipan, an almond and sugar paste, are cute finishing touches.

MAKES 12 CUPCAKES

½ cup (1 stick) plus
2 tablespoons unsalted
butter, cut into chunks

1 cup all-purpose flour

1 cup powdered sugar

¾ teaspoon
baking powder

½ teaspoon baking soda

¼ teaspoon salt

4 large egg whites

Yellow gel paste
food coloring

Honey–Cream Cheese
Frosting (page 108)

**MARZIPAN BEES
(optional)**

2 ounces marzipan

Yellow gel paste
food coloring

Black gel paste
food coloring

Cornstarch, for dusting

Sliced almonds,
for the wings

 Preheat the oven to 350°F. Line a standard 12-cup muffin pan with paper or foil liners.

Place the butter in a medium saucepan and set the pan over medium-low heat. Cook the butter, whisking frequently, until it is deeply browned and smells nutty, 6 to 8 minutes; let cool until barely warm.

In a large bowl, whisk together the flour, powdered sugar, baking powder, baking soda, and salt. Add the egg whites and the cooled butter. Using an electric mixer, mix on medium speed until combined, about 2 minutes. Turn off the mixer and scrape down the sides of the bowl with a rubber spatula.

Divide the batter evenly among the prepared muffin cups. Bake until the tops are light golden brown and a toothpick inserted into the center of a cupcake comes out clean, 18 to 20 minutes. Remove the pan from the oven and set it on a wire rack. Let cool for 10 minutes, then carefully transfer the cupcakes directly to the rack. Let cool completely, about 1 hour.

Add 1 dab of yellow food coloring to the frosting. Using a rubber spatula, mix until the frosting is evenly tinted. Fit a large pastry bag with a plain tip (see page 15; we used Ateco 804), then transfer the frosting to the bag. Pipe tall swirls of frosting onto each cupcake to resemble beehives. Top each beehive with a marzipan bee (if using; see page 94).

1. COLORS To make 12 marzipan bees, divide the marzipan in half. Add 1 dab of yellow food coloring to 1 portion and 1 dab of black food coloring to the other portion. Wearing rubber gloves if you have them, knead the yellow portion of marzipan until it is evenly tinted, then knead the black portion until it is evenly tinted. Pinch off and reserve a small piece of the yellow marzipan to use for the eyes.

2. STRIPES Dust a clean work surface with cornstarch, then roll each portion of marzipan into a rope about ¼ inch thick.

3. BODIES Cut the rope crosswise into ¼-inch pieces. Alternating yellow and black, lay 4 pieces next to each other and gently press them together.

4. EYES Pinch off 2 tiny pieces of the reserved yellow marzipan and roll each into a small ball, then press the pieces onto the black piece on the end.

5. WINGS Insert 1 almond slice into each side of the body to form the wings.

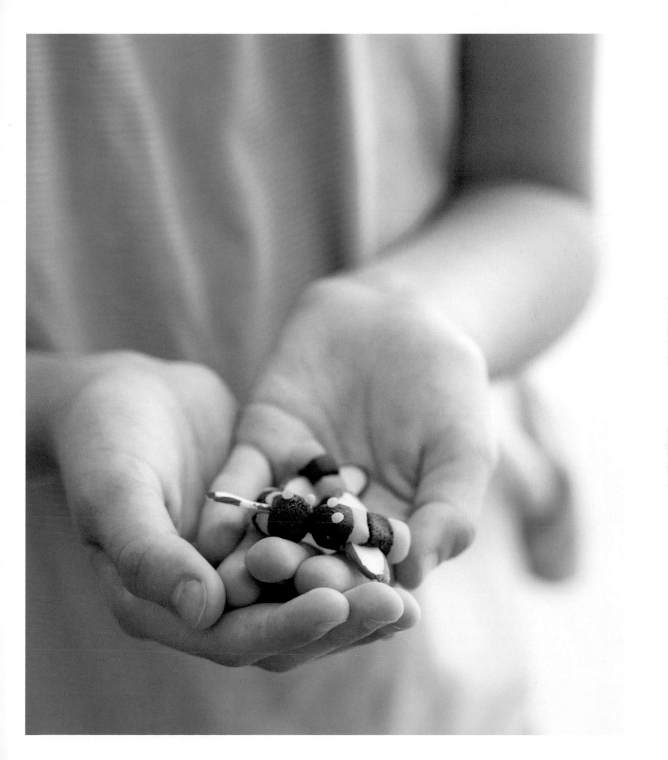

Spooky sweets
A toothpick or wooden skewer makes it easy to create this super-fun Halloween-inspired spiderweb pattern.

Pumpkin-Chocolate Chip Cupcakes

When you think of pumpkins, you think of Halloween, right? These spiced chocolate chip–studded cupcakes are decorated with an easy-to-make chocolate and vanilla spiderweb design—all you need is a toothpick to create the pretty pattern!

MAKES 12 CUPCAKES

1 cup all-purpose flour

1 teaspoon baking powder

½ teaspoon baking soda

¼ teaspoon salt

1 teaspoon ground cinnamon

½ teaspoon ground ginger

¼ teaspoon ground allspice

Pinch of ground nutmeg

1 cup canned pumpkin purée

1 cup sugar

½ cup vegetable oil

2 large eggs

1 cup mini semisweet chocolate chips

Rich Chocolate Glaze (page 114)

Vanilla Glaze (page 114)

 Preheat the oven to 350°F. Line a standard 12-cup muffin pan with paper or foil liners.

In a medium bowl, whisk together the flour, baking powder, baking soda, salt, cinnamon, ginger, allspice, and nutmeg. In a large bowl, whisk together the pumpkin purée, sugar, oil, and eggs. Add the flour mixture and whisk until well combined. Using a rubber spatula, fold in the chocolate chips.

Divide the batter evenly among the prepared muffin cups. Bake until a toothpick inserted into the center of a cupcake comes out clean, 22 to 24 minutes. Remove the pan from the oven and set it on a wire rack. Let cool for 10 minutes, then carefully transfer the cupcakes directly to the rack. Let cool completely, about 1 hour.

Spoon the chocolate glaze over the cupcakes. To make spiderweb designs, fit a small pastry bag with a small plain tip (see page 15), then transfer the vanilla glaze to the bag. Pipe concentric circles of vanilla glaze onto a chocolate-glazed cupcake. Lightly draw the tip of a toothpick or wooden skewer from the center of the cupcake outward to the edge, spacing the lines evenly and occasionally alternating the direction. For the cleanest look, wipe the tip of the toothpick or skewer after each draw. Repeat with the remaining cupcakes. Let the glaze dry for about 30 minutes.

Cinnamon Roll Cupcakes

These cinnamon rolls baked in a muffin pan are so rich and buttery—and so yummy with their cream cheese frosting—that they're as great for dessert as they are for breakfast or brunch. The dough needs to rise twice, so be sure to plan ahead.

MAKES 24 CUPCAKES

DOUGH

1 cup whole milk

½ cup granulated sugar

5 tablespoons unsalted butter, melted, plus more for greasing the bowl

3 large eggs

1 package (about 2¼ teaspoons) quick-rise yeast

4½ cups all-purpose flour, plus more as needed

1¼ teaspoons salt

FILLING

1½ cups firmly packed light brown sugar

4 teaspoons ground cinnamon

½ cup (1 stick) unsalted butter, at room temperature

Cream Cheese Frosting (page 108)

To make the dough, in the bowl of a stand mixer, whisk the milk, sugar, melted butter, eggs, and yeast until blended. Add the flour and salt. Attach the bowl to the mixer and fit the mixer with the paddle attachment. Beat on medium-low speed until the mixture forms a soft dough that does not stick to the bowl, about 1 minute; add up to ½ cup more flour if the dough is very sticky. Turn off the mixer. Remove the paddle attachment and fit the mixer with the dough hook attachment. Knead the dough on medium-low speed, adding more flour if needed, until the dough is smooth but still soft, 6 to 7 minutes. Turn off the mixer.

Brush a large bowl with melted butter. Remove the dough from the mixer bowl and set it on a clean work surface. Using your hands, shape it into a ball. Place the dough in the prepared bowl and turn it to coat its entire surface with butter. Cover with plastic wrap and let rise in a warm place until the dough has doubled in size, 2 to 2½ hours.

Meanwhile, make the filling: In a clean stand mixer bowl, add the brown sugar, cinnamon, and butter. Fit the mixer with the paddle attachment and attach the bowl to the mixer. Beat on low speed just until the mixture comes together but is still crumbly, about 30 seconds. Set aside.

Line two standard 12-cup muffin pans with paper or foil liners.

When the dough has doubled in size, use your hand to gently punch down and deflate it. Lightly flour a clean work surface. Turn the dough out onto the

Prep step

After shaping and cutting, this dough can be refrigerated for up to 12 hours, so you can do most of the work in advance.

floured surface and dust the top with flour. Using a rolling pin, roll out the dough to a 16-by-14-inch rectangle, with a long side facing you. Cut the dough in half crosswise so that you have two 8-by-14-inch pieces.

Sprinkle half of the filling evenly over one piece of the dough, leaving a 1-inch border at the top and bottom. Starting at the long side of the rectangle nearest you, roll up the rectangle into a log, then pinch the seam to seal. Repeat with the second piece of dough. Using a sharp knife, trim 1 inch off each end of each log using a sawing motion; discard the ends. Cut each log in half crosswise, then cut each half into 6 pieces, each about 1 inch thick. Place each piece, cut side up so that the swirl is visible, in a prepared muffin cup. Cover loosely with plastic wrap and let rise in a warm place until the rolls have doubled in size, 1½ to 2 hours. (Or you can refrigerate the dough in the muffin pans for 8 to 12 hours; remove from the refrigerator 1 hour before baking.)

Meanwhile, preheat the oven to 350°F. Bake until the rolls are golden brown, 20 to 22 minutes. Remove the pans from the oven and set them on a wire rack. Let cool for 15 minutes, then carefully transfer the rolls directly to the wire rack. Let cool for at least 15 minutes more before frosting.

Using a small icing spatula or a butter knife, or a pastry bag fitted with a plain tip (see page 15), top the cupcakes with the frosting. Serve slightly warm or at room temperature.

Peppermint Bark Cupcakes

Chocolate-glazed minty cupcakes topped with white chocolate and crushed peppermint candies are perfect for winter parties. To crush the candies, place them in a zipper-lock bag, seal the bag, then use a rolling pin or wooden spoon to crush the candies.

MAKES 12 CUPCAKES

1¼ cups all-purpose flour

1¼ teaspoons
baking powder

¼ teaspoon salt

1 cup sugar

6 tablespoons (¾ stick)
unsalted butter,
at room temperature

2 large eggs

½ teaspoon
peppermint extract

½ cup whole milk

4 ounces white
chocolate, chopped

Rich Chocolate Glaze
(page 114)

¾ cup crushed
peppermint candies

 Preheat the oven to 350°F. Line a standard 12-cup muffin pan with paper or foil liners.

In a medium bowl, whisk together the flour, baking powder, and salt. In another bowl, using an electric mixer, beat the sugar and butter on medium-high speed until light and fluffy, 2 to 3 minutes. Add the eggs one at a time, beating well after each addition. Turn off the mixer and scrape down the bowl with a rubber spatula. Add the peppermint extract and beat until combined. Add half of the flour mixture and mix on low speed just until blended. Pour in the milk and mix on low speed just until combined. Add the remaining flour mixture and mix on low speed just until blended. Turn off the mixer, scrape down the bowl, and give the batter a final stir with the spatula.

Divide the batter evenly among the prepared muffin cups. Bake until light golden brown and a toothpick inserted into the center of a cupcake comes out clean, 18 to 20 minutes. Remove the pan from the oven and set it on a wire rack. Let cool for 10 minutes, then carefully transfer the cupcakes directly to the rack. Let cool completely, about 1 hour.

Place the white chocolate in a small microwave-safe bowl. Microwave on high power, stirring every 20 seconds, until the chocolate is melted and smooth.

Spoon the chocolate glaze over each cupcake, then sprinkle with the crushed peppermint candies. Using a small spoon, drizzle the white chooclate on top.

Frostings, Glazes & More

Fluffy Vanilla Frosting

This versatile frosting is delicious paired with almost any cupcake in this book. And it's a great base for flavor variations such as mint, white chocolate, raspberry, and coconut; see variations below.

½ cup (1 stick) unsalted butter, at room temperature

2½ cups powdered sugar

3 tablespoons whole milk

1 teaspoon vanilla extract

Pinch of salt

In a large bowl, using an electric mixer, beat the butter on medium speed until light and fluffy, about 2 minutes. Turn off the mixer. Add the powdered sugar, milk, vanilla, and salt. Mix on low speed just until combined. Stop the mixer and scrape down the bowl with a rubber spatula. Beat on medium-high speed until the frosting is airy and smooth, about 5 minutes.

Frosting Variations

Fluffy Mint Frosting: Add ½ teaspoon peppermint extract along with the sugar, milk, vanilla, and salt.

Fluffy Coconut Frosting: Add 1 teaspoon coconut extract along with the sugar, milk, vanilla, and salt.

Fluffy Raspberry Frosting: Follow the recipe for Fluffy Vanilla Frosting. Place 1 cup raspberries into a fine-mesh strainer. Holding the strainer over the bowl of frosting, press the raspberries with a rubber spatula to extract as much juice as you can; discard the seeds and pulp. Gently fold the raspberry juices into the frosting with the rubber spatula until no streaks remain.

Fluffy White Chocolate Frosting: Place 4 ounces white chocolate, finely chopped, in a small microwave-safe bowl. Microwave on high power, stirring every 20 seconds, just until the chocolate is melted and smooth. Let the white chocolate cool slightly. Follow the recipe for Fluffy Vanilla Frosting, add the melted white chocolate, then beat on medium-high speed until well combined.

Sweetened Whipped Cream

Whipped cream is a super-simple topping for cupcakes. If you use a chilled bowl and beaters, the cream will whip up quickly and with lots of volume. Once whipped, the cream gradually deflates, so make it just before you use it.

MAKES ABOUT 1½ CUPS

1 cup cold heavy cream

2 tablespoons powdered sugar

In a chilled medium bowl, combine the cream and sugar. Using an electric mixer, beat the mixture on low speed until slightly thickened, 1 to 2 minutes. Gradually increase the speed to medium-high and continue to beat until the cream holds soft peaks when the beaters are lifted, 2 to 3 minutes. Use right away.

Cream Cheese Frosting

Sweet and slightly tangy, cream cheese frosting pairs well with many different types of cupcakes; see variations below. If you will be piping this frosting instead of spreading it, double the amount of powdered sugar to make it easier to work with in the piping bag.

MAKES ABOUT 1½ CUPS

1 (8-ounce) package cream cheese, at room temperature

6 tablespoons (¾ stick) unsalted butter, at room temperature

1 teaspoon vanilla extract

1 cup powdered sugar (plus 1 cup if you will be using a piping bag)

In a large bowl, using an electric mixer, beat the cream cheese, butter, and vanilla on medium-high speed until light and fluffy, about 2 minutes. Turn off the mixer and scrape down the bowl with a rubber spatula. Add about half of the powdered sugar and mix on low speed until well blended. Turn off the mixer, add the remaining sugar, and beat on medium speed until smooth. The frosting should be spreadable; if it is too soft, cover the bowl and refrigerate it for about 15 minutes.

Frosting Variations

Honey–Cream Cheese Frosting:
Add 3 tablespoons honey with the cream cheese, butter, and vanilla.

Coconut–Cream Cheese Frosting:
Add 1½ teaspoons coconut extract with the cream cheese, butter, and vanilla.

Strawberry–Cream Cheese Frosting:
Place ½ cup freeze-dried strawberries (see page 34) in a quart-size zipper-lock bag and seal the bag. Using a rolling pin or wooden spoon, crush the strawberries to a fine powder. Follow the recipe for Cream Cheese Frosting, then turn off the mixer. Add the strawberry powder and mix on low speed until well combined.

Blackberry–Cream Cheese Frosting:
Follow the recipe for Cream Cheese Frosting, then turn off the mixer. Add ½ cup blackberry jam and mix on low speed until well combined.

Marshmallow Frosting

This frosting requires cooking at the stovetop, so ask an adult for help. An instant-read thermometer indicates when the egg whites are properly heated so they don't overcook. Make sure the mixture is warm when you add the marshmallows so that they fully melt.

MAKES ABOUT 5 CUPS

2 large egg whites

1 cup sugar

6 tablespoons water

1 tablespoon light corn syrup

½ teaspoon cream of tartar

Pinch of salt

1 cup miniature marshmallows

1 teaspoon vanilla extract

Select a saucepan and a large heatproof bowl that fits snugly on top of the pan. Fill the pan one-third full of water, making sure the water doesn't touch the bottom of the bowl when the bowl is placed on top. Bring the water to a gentle simmer over medium heat.

Combine the egg whites, sugar, water, corn syrup, cream of tartar, and salt in the bowl. Set the bowl on top of the saucepan and heat the mixture, whisking constantly, until the sugar dissolves and the mixture is very warm to the touch (about 160°F on an instant-read thermometer), about 2 minutes. Very carefully remove the bowl from the saucepan.

Using an electric mixer, beat the mixture on medium-high speed until it is warm and holds soft peaks when the beaters are lifted, about 2 minutes. Turn off the mixer and add the marshmallows and vanilla. Beat on low speed until the marshmallows are melted and the frosting is completely smooth, about 2 minutes.

Peanut Butter Frosting

If you thought peanut butter couldn't get any better, try this super-simple frosting. For really rich, extra-nutty flavor, use natural or old-fashioned peanut butter, but make sure to stir it well before measuring because the oil naturally separates to the top.

MAKES ABOUT 1½ CUPS

6 tablespoons (¾ stick) unsalted butter, at room temperature

¾ cup powdered sugar

¾ cup smooth peanut butter

¼ cup heavy cream

In a large bowl, using an electric mixer, beat the butter, powdered sugar, peanut butter, and cream on medium-low speed until smooth and combined, about 2 minutes. Turn off the mixer and scrape down the bowl with a rubber spatula as needed.

Chocolate Frosting

This rich and buttery chocolate frosting is so delicious you'll want to eat it from the bowl. No one will notice if you sneak a spoonful or two, but try to save most of it for frosting your cupcakes!

MAKES ABOUT 3 CUPS

3½ cups powdered sugar

1 cup unsweetened cocoa powder

½ cup (1 stick) unsalted butter, cut into 8 pieces, at room temperature

1 teaspoon vanilla extract

Pinch of salt

1 cup heavy cream, plus more as needed

Sift the powdered sugar and cocoa into a large bowl. Add the butter. Using an electric mixer, beat the mixture on low speed just until crumbly. Add the vanilla and salt and beat until combined. Turn off the mixer. Add the cream and beat on medium speed until the frosting is smooth, about 1 minute. The frosting should be smooth and spreadable; if it is too thick, beat in more cream 1 teaspoon at a time until it reaches the proper consistency.

Rich Chocolate Glaze

This smooth, shiny, very chocolaty glaze can be used as a filling or as a topping. Let the glaze cool a bit before you use it; it should be warm if used for a filling, or cooled to room temperature if used as a topping, otherwise it'll be too thin to coat the cupcakes.

MAKES ABOUT 1¾ CUPS

1 cup heavy cream

1 tablespoon light corn syrup

Pinch of salt

8 ounces semisweet chocolate, chopped

In a medium saucepan, combine the cream, corn syrup, and salt. Set the pan over medium-high heat and bring to a simmer, stirring occasionally. Remove the pan from the heat, add the chocolate, and let stand for about 3 minutes.

Using a wooden spoon, stir until the chocolate is completely melted and the mixture is smooth. Let cool until warm if using the glaze as a filling; let cool to room temperature if using as a topping.

(The cooled glaze can be refrigerated in an airtight container for up to 3 days. Before using, soften the glaze by gently heating it in a heatproof bowl set over, but not touching, simmering water in a saucepan.)

Vanilla & Lemon Glazes

Vanilla Glaze: In a small bowl, whisk together 1 cup powdered sugar, 2 tablespoons whole milk, and 1 teaspoon vanilla extract until smooth; the glaze should be spreadable but not runny. If it is too thick, whisk in additional milk a few drops at a time; if it is too thin, whisk in additional sugar 1 teaspoon at a time.

Lemon Glaze: Substitute fresh lemon juice for the milk and 2 teaspoons grated lemon zest for the vanilla.

Vanilla Custard

This creamy cupcake filling is so yummy that you'll want to eat it with a spoon. It's also great spread between layers of cake or piped into cream puffs. Straining after cooking removes any lumps so that it's sure to be silky and smooth.

MAKES ABOUT 2½ CUPS

4 large egg yolks

½ cup sugar

¼ cup cornstarch

¼ teaspoon salt

2 cups whole milk

1½ teaspoons vanilla extract

In a medium bowl, whisk the egg yolks and set aside.

In a medium saucepan, whisk together the sugar, cornstarch, and salt. Slowly whisk in the milk and vanilla. Set the pan over medium heat and bring the mixture to a simmer, stirring occasionally to start but constantly as the mixture comes close to a simmer and thickens. Remove the pan from the heat.

While whisking constantly, add about one-third of the hot thickened milk mixture to the egg yolks. Now whisk the egg yolk mixture into the hot milk mixture in the saucepan. Set the pan over medium heat and cook, stirring constantly, until the pastry cream reaches a simmer and thickens, about 4 minutes. Continue to cook, whisking constantly, for about 1 minute longer. The custard should be thick enough to coat the back of a spoon. Remove from the heat.

Set a medium-mesh strainer over a medium bowl and pour the pastry cream into the strainer. Using a rubber spatula, stir and push the pastry cream through the strainer, then scrape the bottom of the strainer to collect as much of the pastry cream as you can. Press a piece of plastic wrap directly against the surface of the pastry cream to prevent a skin from forming. Let cool for 15 minutes.

(The custard can be stored in the refrigerator in an airtight container for up to 2 days.)

Caramel Drizzle

A drizzle of thick, rich caramel makes even the simplest cupcakes look and taste special. Sugar becomes very hot and sticky when made into caramel, so ask an adult for help. Watch the sugar as it cooks because once it starts to turn brown, it darkens very quickly.

MAKES ABOUT 2½ CUPS

1½ cups sugar

1¼ cups heavy cream

Pinch of salt

Place the sugar in a heavy-bottomed, high-sided medium saucepan and set the pan over medium-high heat. Cook the sugar until it begins to melt around the edges, about 5 minutes. Stir with a clean wooden spoon and continue to cook until the sugar is melted and has turned golden brown in color, about 3 minutes longer.

Carefully pour the cream down the inside of the pan in a slow, steady stream—be very careful because the mixture will bubble and spatter! Continue to cook over medium heat, stirring constantly, until the caramel is completely smooth. Remove the pan from the heat and stir in the salt. Pour the caramel into a small heatproof bowl and let cool completely.

(The caramel can be refrigerated in an airtight container for up to 1 week; bring to room temperature before using.)

Crumb Topping

This buttery, crumbly topping turns irresistibly crunchy during baking atop Apple Crumb Cupcakes (page 50). You could also use it to jazz up simple vanilla, yellow, or even gingerbread cupcakes.

MAKES ABOUT 2 CUPS

1¼ cups all-purpose flour

½ cup firmly packed light brown sugar

1½ teaspoons ground cinnamon

¼ teaspoon salt

¾ cup (1½ sticks) unsalted butter, at room temperature

In a medium bowl, whisk together the flour, brown sugar, cinnamon, and salt. Add the butter and, using a fork, mash it into the flour mixture until large, moist crumbs form.

Better butter
Be gentle when using a fork to incorporate the softened butter into the topping. Only mix until large crumbs form.

Sugared Flowers

To make sugared flowers, use organic, edible flowers that have not been sprayed with pesticides, and make sure that the flowers are completely dry before you brush them. Two tablespoons of pasteurized egg whites can be used in place of the raw egg white.

MAKES 24 SUGARED FLOWERS

1 large egg white

A few drops of water

24 organic edible flowers, such as violets, pansies, and rose petals

Superfine sugar, for sprinkling

 Line a rimmed cookie sheet with parchment paper and set it aside.

In a small bowl, whisk the egg white and water until foamy. Using a small, clean paintbrush, lightly coat each flower or petal completely with the egg white mixture.

Sprinkle the coated flowers or petals evenly with sugar, covering them completely. Place them in a single layer on the prepared baking sheet and let stand at room temperature until the egg white is dry, about 1 hour.

Store the sugared flowers in an airtight container at room temperature for up to 1 hour.

Index

weldonowen

1045 Sansome Street, Suite 100
San Francisco, CA 94111
www.weldonowen.com

WELDON OWEN
President & Publisher Roger Shaw
SVP, Sales & Marketing Amy Kaneko

Associate Publisher Amy Marr
Project Editor Alexis Mersel

Creative Director Kelly Booth
Designer Lisa Berman
Original Design Alexandra Zeigler

Production Director Michelle Duggan
Imaging Manager Don Hill

Photographer Nicole Hill Gerulat
Food Stylist Tara Bench
Wardrobe & Prop Stylists Veronica Olson
Hair & Makeup Kathy Hill

AMERICAN GIRL *CUPCAKES*
Conceived and produced by Weldon Owen.

A WELDON OWEN PRODUCTION

Printed and bound in China

First printed in 2018
10 9 8 7 6 5 4 3 2 1

Library of Congress Cataloging in Publication
data is available

ISBN: 978-1-68188-453-0

ACKNOWLEDGMENTS
Weldon Owen wishes to thank the following people for their generous support to help produce this book:
Mary Bench, Lesley Bruynesteyn, Lou Bustamante, Lindsey Hargett, Rachel Markowitz, Taylor Olson,
Elizabeth Parson, Reagan Tidwell, Nathalie Van Emplin, and Dawn Yanagihara

A VERY SPECIAL THANK YOU TO:
Our models: Kaylyn Cox, Evie Gerulat, Jane Jensen, Adyson Kandell, and Leimana Paea

Our locations: The Gerulat Family

Collect Them All

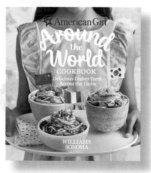